Hello, Artistic Carbon-based Life-forms. (Yes, that means YOU!)

Growing up in the 1960s and '70s, I was fascinated by the robots I saw in movies and on television. They were not the slick, high-tech robots that you see today. They were hulking, clumsy machines—impressively frightening yet really cool to me as a kid.

In this book I hope to share my love for these mechanized creatures by showing you some simple ways to draw your own. You can start by using geometric shapes and lines to draw a basic robot. You can then add parts from the Spare Parts Warehouse to make your creation unique. From there, I'll show you some robot designs, which I hope will spark your imagination.

Follow the steps in red to create your robots. Then color in your artwork with your favorite tools. You'll also find some blue challenge steps for even more fun with your drawings.

If you can draw a square, a circle, and a rectangle, you can draw a ROBOT!

Ralph

Choose your tools

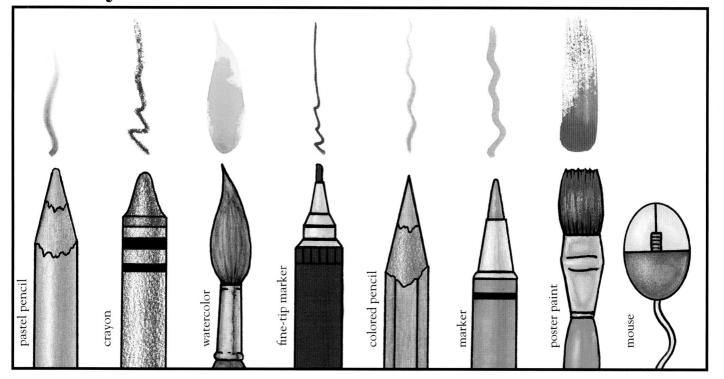

pastel pencil

crayon

watercolor

fine-tip marker

colored pencil

marker

poster paint

mouse

Shapes

You can use any and all shapes to draw your robots.

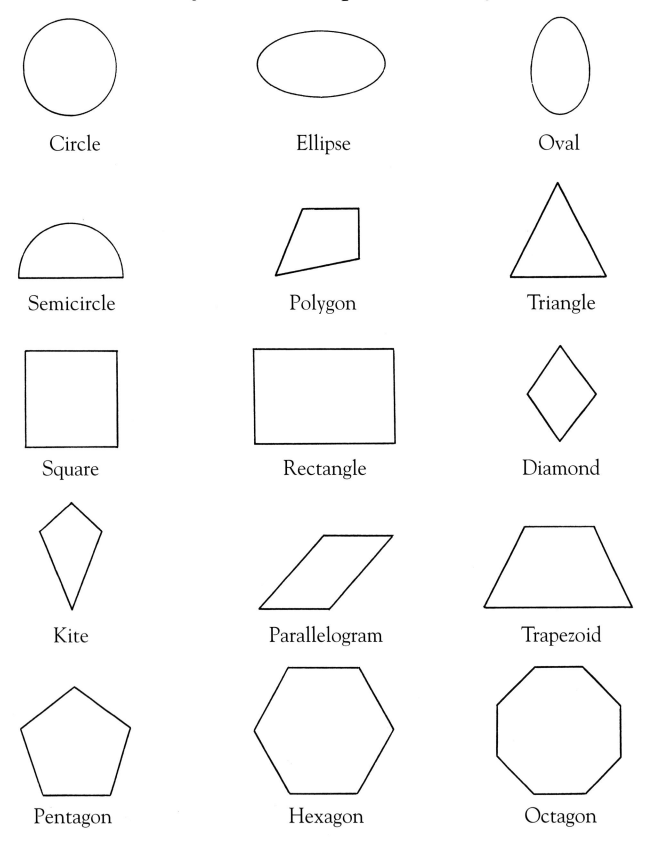

Circle	Ellipse	Oval
Semicircle	Polygon	Triangle
Square	Rectangle	Diamond
Kite	Parallelogram	Trapezoid
Pentagon	Hexagon	Octagon

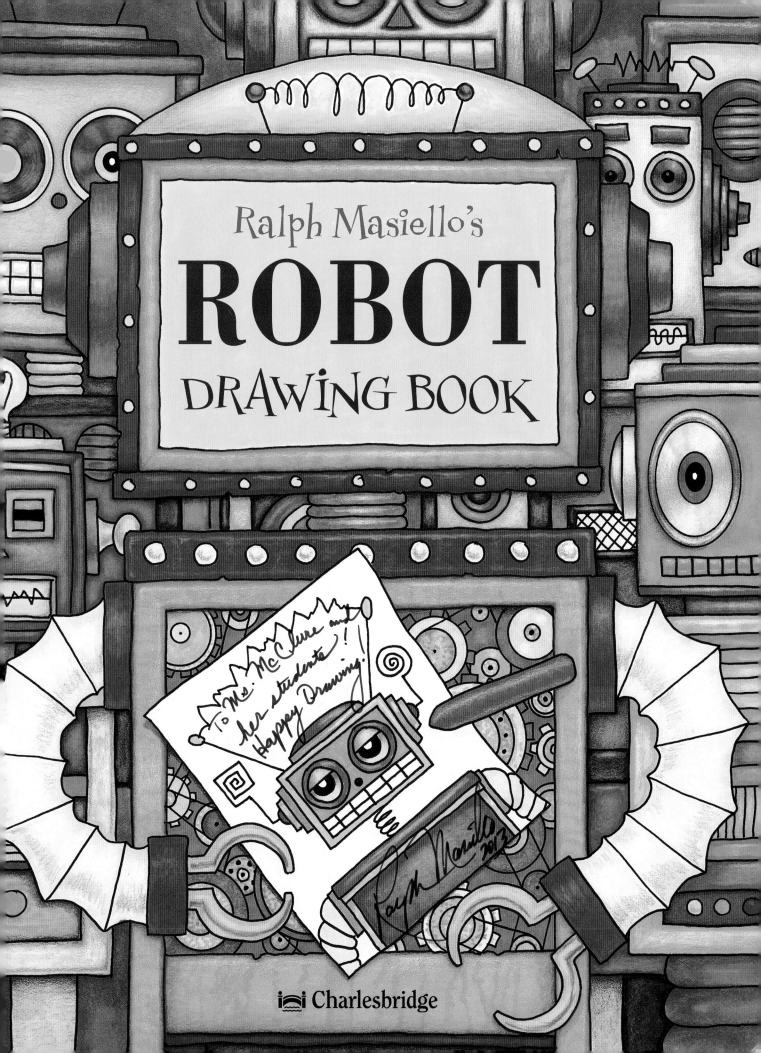

For art teachers everywhere, who make the human world more human through art—R. M.

Also in this series:
Ralph Masiello's Ancient Egypt Drawing Book
Ralph Masiello's Bug Drawing Book
Ralph Masiello's Dinosaur Drawing Book
Ralph Masiello's Dragon Drawing Book
Ralph Masiello's Ocean Drawing Book

Other books illustrated by Ralph Masiello:
The Dinosaur Alphabet Book
The Extinct Alphabet Book
The Flag We Love
The Frog Alphabet Book
The Icky Bug Alphabet Book
The Icky Bug Counting Book
The Skull Alphabet Book
The Yucky Reptile Alphabet Book
Cuenta los insectos

Published by Charlesbridge
85 Main Street
Watertown, MA 02472
(617) 926-0329
www.charlesbridge.com

Library of Congress Cataloging-in-Publication Data
Masiello, Ralph.
  Ralph Masiello's robot drawing book / Ralph Masiello.
    p. cm.
  ISBN 978-1-57091-535-2 (reinforced for library use)
  ISBN 978-1-57091-536-9 (softcover)
1. Robots in art—Juvenile literature. 2. Drawing—Technique—Juvenile
literature. I. Title. II. Title: Robot drawing book.
NC825.R56M37 2011
743'.89629892—dc22   2010033634

Printed in China
(hc) 10 9 8 7 6 5 4 3 2 1
(sc) 10 9 8 7 6 5 4 3 2 1

Illustrations done in mixed media
Display type set in Couchlover, designed by Chank, Minneapolis, Minnesota;
    text type set in Goudy
Color separations by Chroma Graphics, Singapore
Printed and bound February 2011 by Jade Productions in Heyuan,
    Guangdong, China
Production supervision by Brian G. Walker
Designed by Susan Mallory Sherman and Martha MacLeod Sikkema

Lines

Here are some lines you can use on your robotic creations.

Straight

Wavy

Zigzag

Springy

Crosshatched

Crisscrossed

Spiral   Square Spiral   Stepped

Simplibot

Claws

Round

Square

I salute you, friend of robots!

digital

Spare Parts Warehouse

Use these to upgrade your robots.

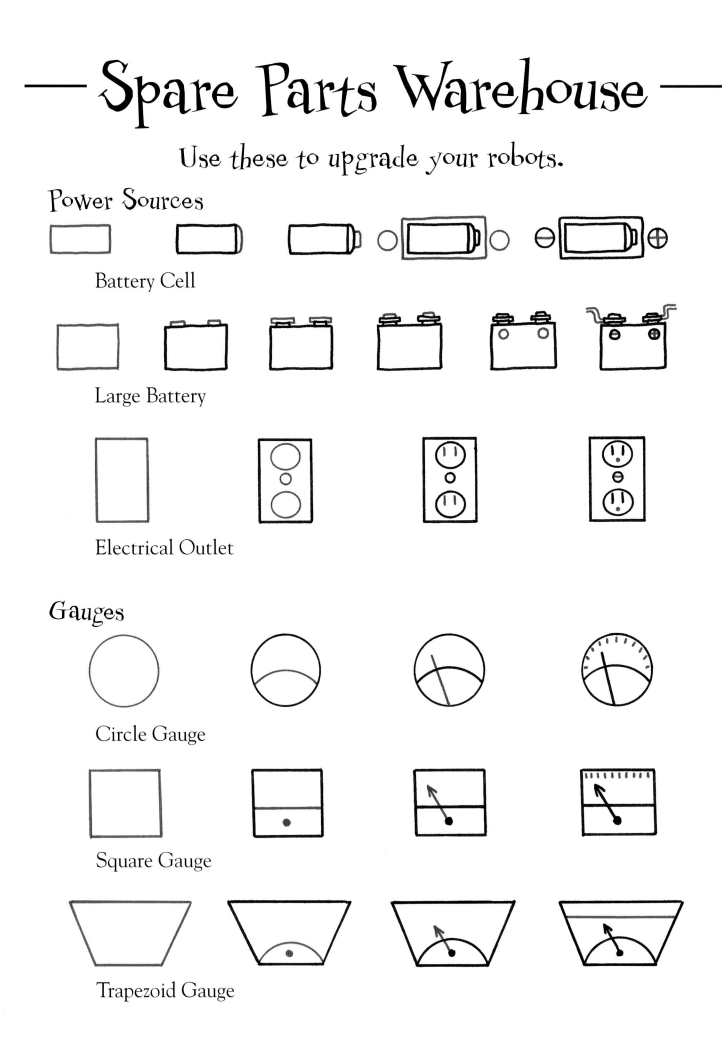

Power Sources

Battery Cell

Large Battery

Electrical Outlet

Gauges

Circle Gauge

Square Gauge

Trapezoid Gauge

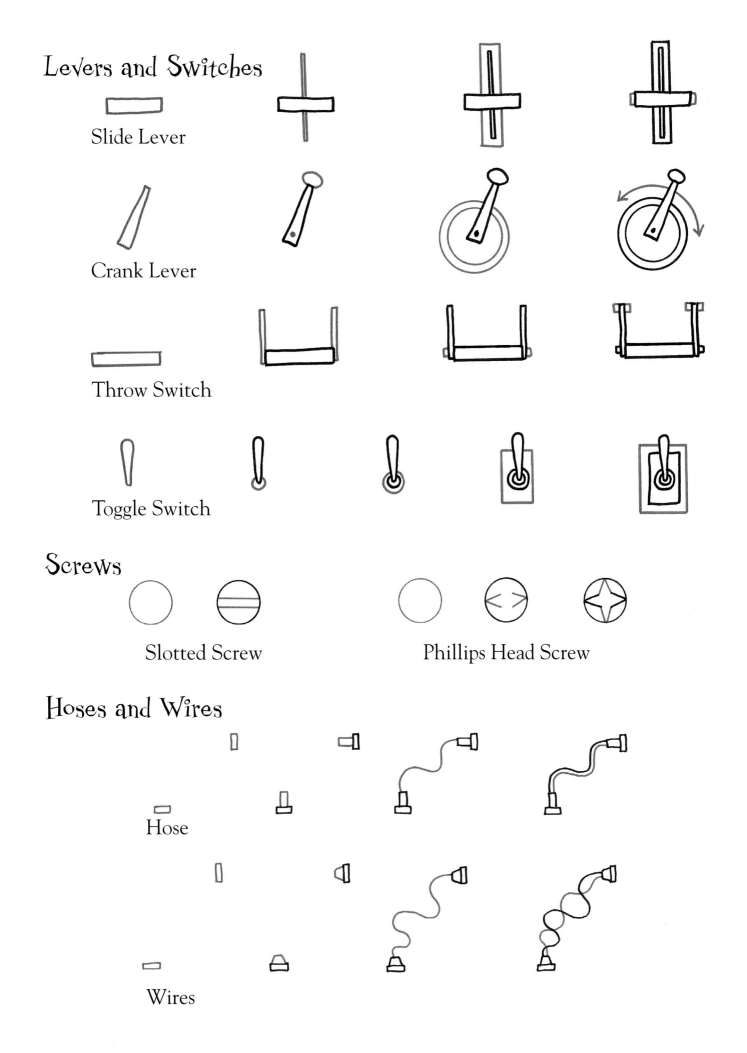

Levers and Switches

Slide Lever

Crank Lever

Throw Switch

Toggle Switch

Screws

Slotted Screw

Phillips Head Screw

Hoses and Wires

Hose

Wires

Antennae

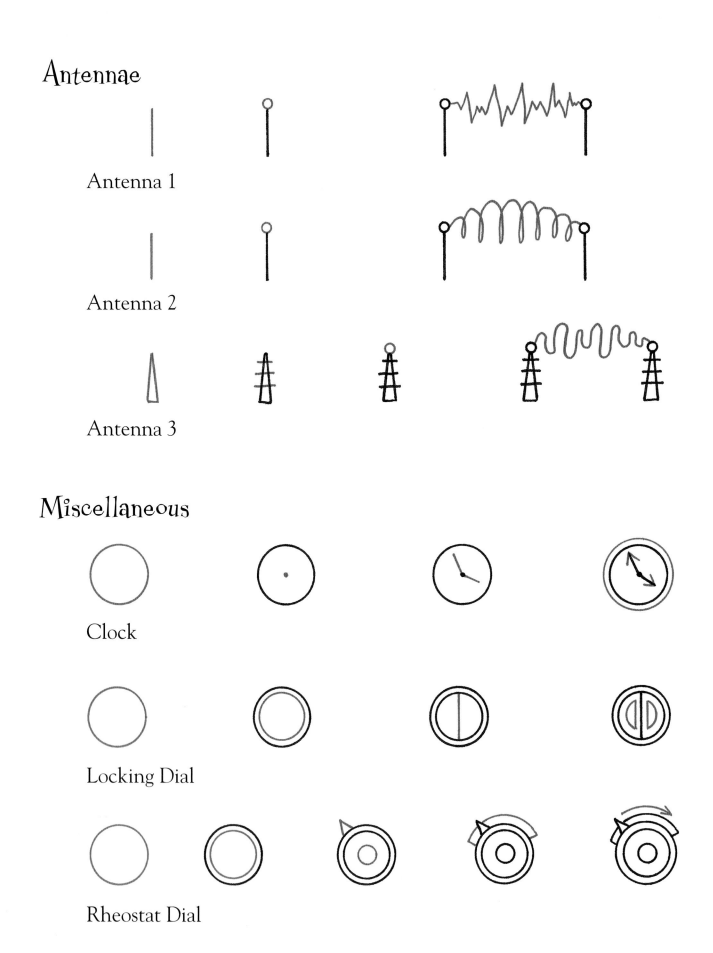

Antenna 1

Antenna 2

Antenna 3

Miscellaneous

Clock

Locking Dial

Rheostat Dial

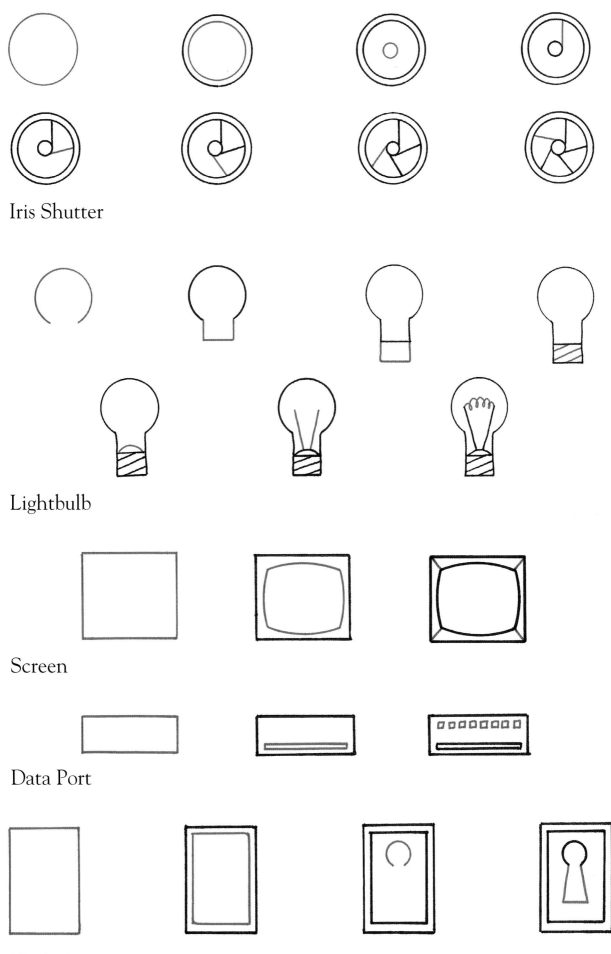

Iris Shutter

Lightbulb

Screen

Data Port

Keyhole

Squarehead Thinbot

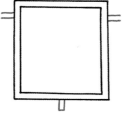
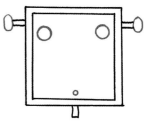

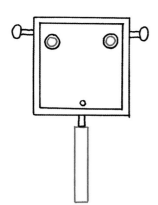
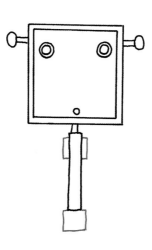
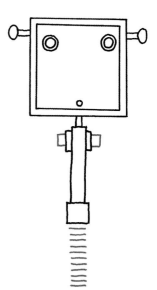

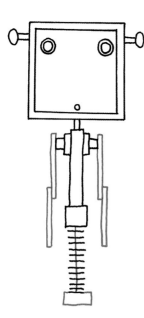
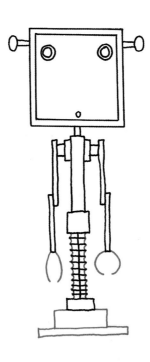
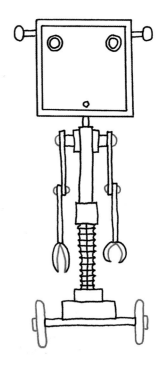

Spare parts are a must.
(Gee, I hope I don't rust.)

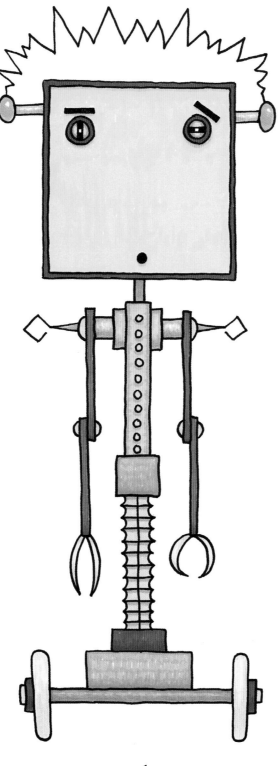

marker

Sparky Springbot

I get a "charge" out of drawing!

crayon

Saucerbot

  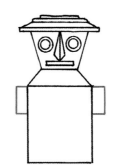 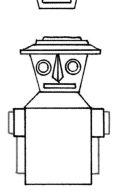

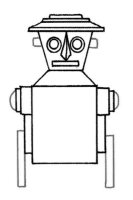 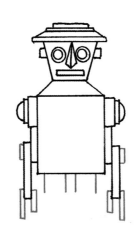 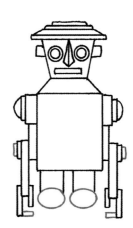 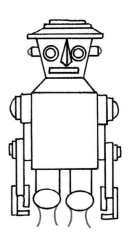

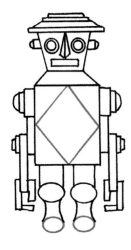 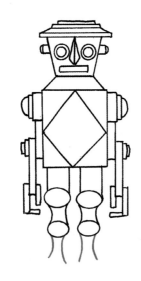 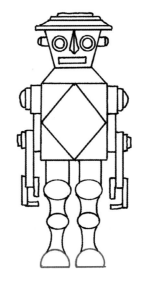 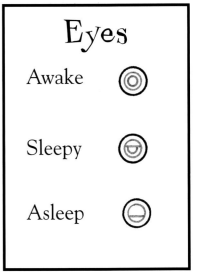

Eyes

Awake

Sleepy

Asleep

Powering down.

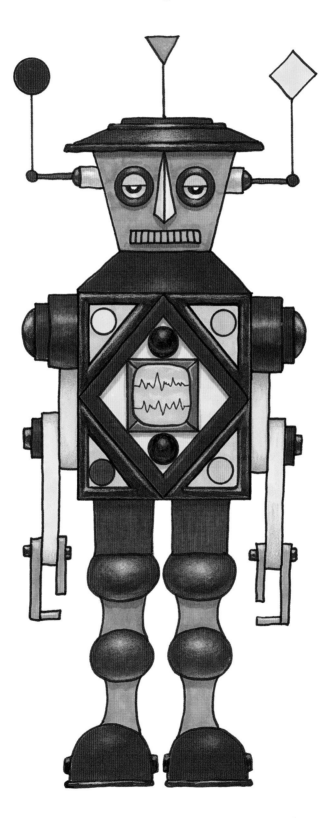

marker and colored pencil

Bakerbot

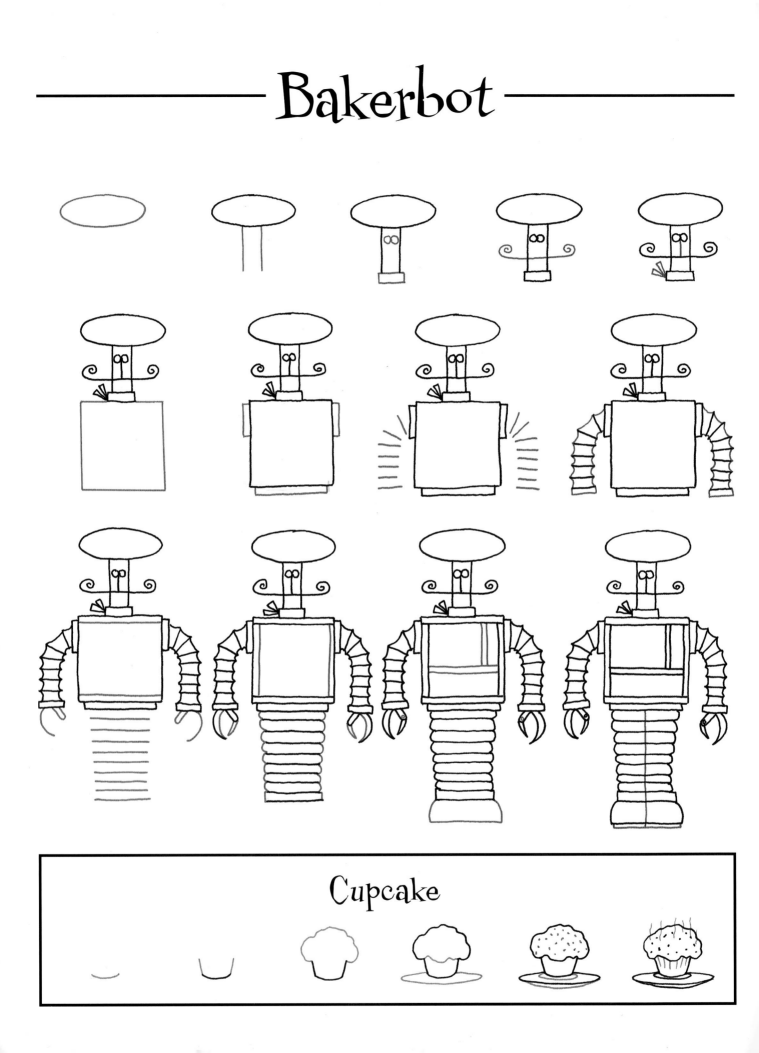

Cupcake

Cooking up some great ideas.

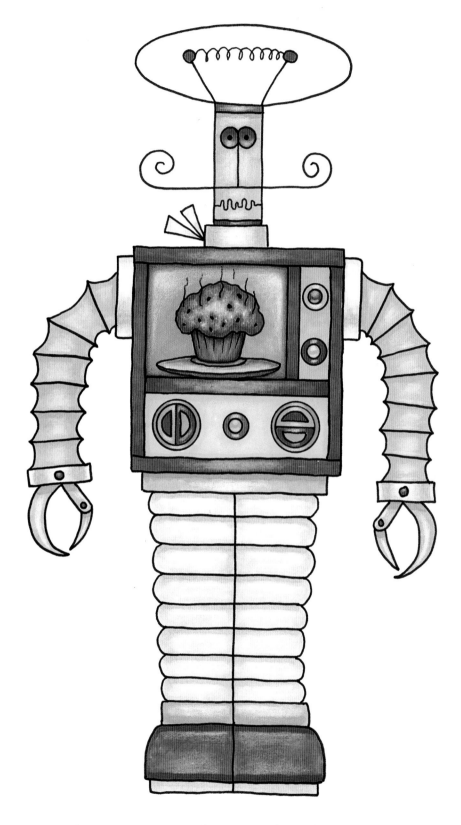

marker, watercolor, and colored pencil

Zoidbot

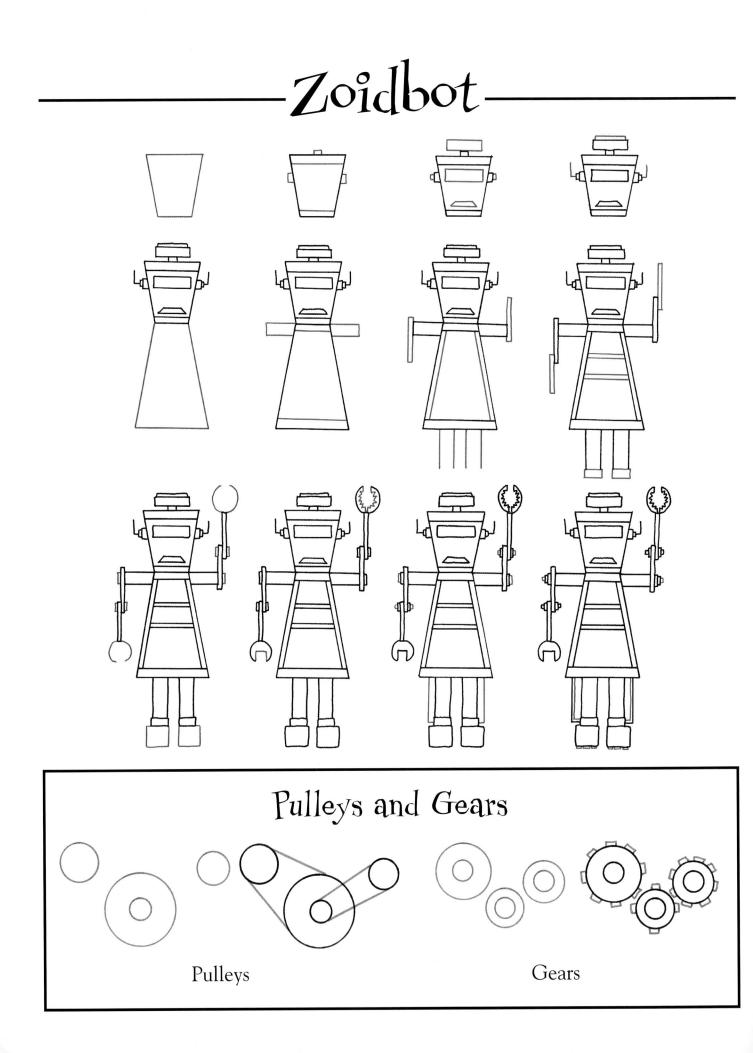

Pulleys and Gears

Pulleys

Gears

Mechanized mayhem!

marker, poster paint, and colored pencil

Pentabot

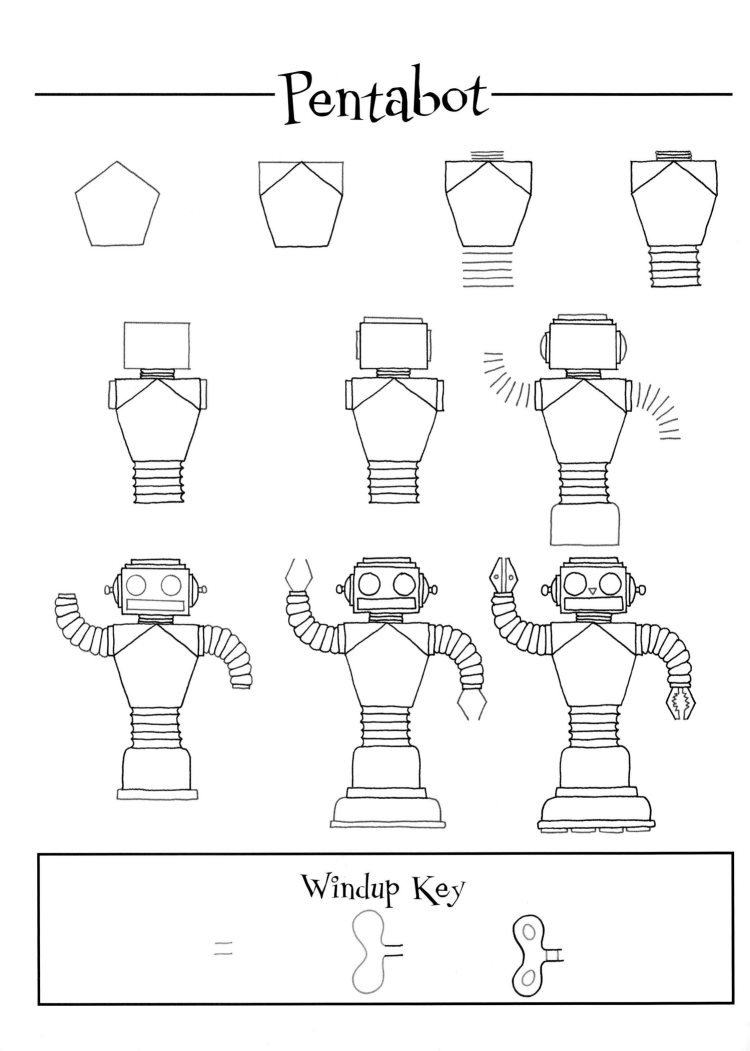

Windup Key

Wind me up before you go-go.

marker and pastel pencil

Ovalbot

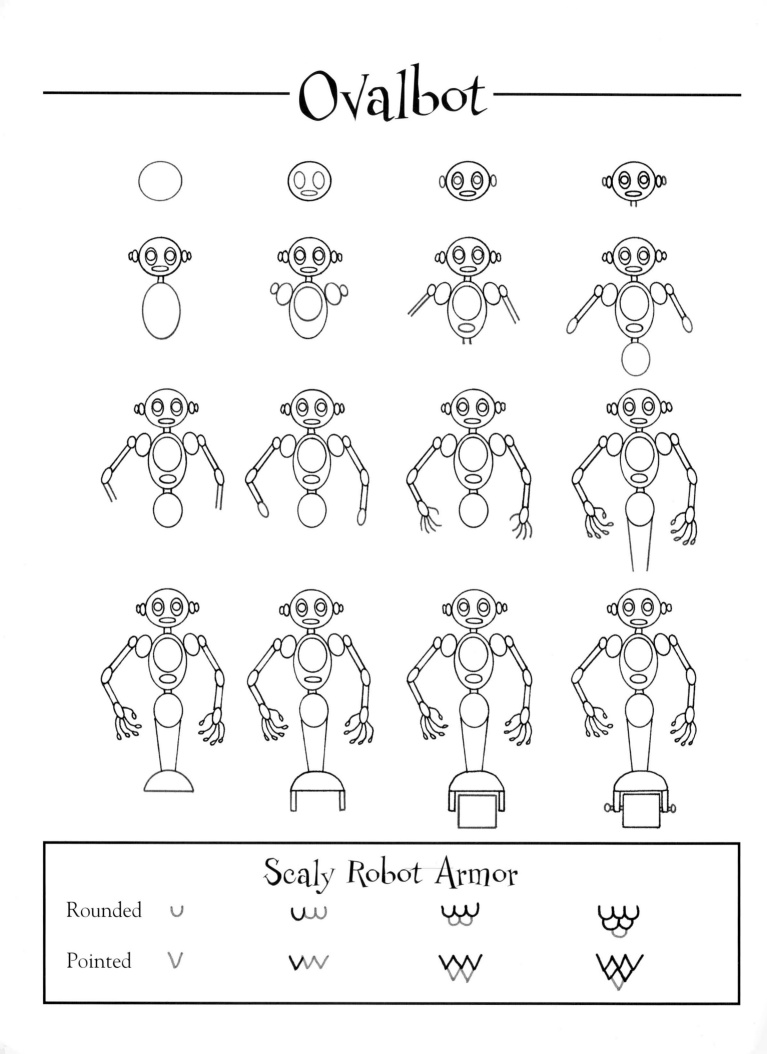

Scaly Robot Armor

Rounded	∪	ᴡᴡ	ᴡᴡᴡ	ᴡᴡᴡ
Pointed	V	VVV	VVV	VVVV

Now we're rolling!

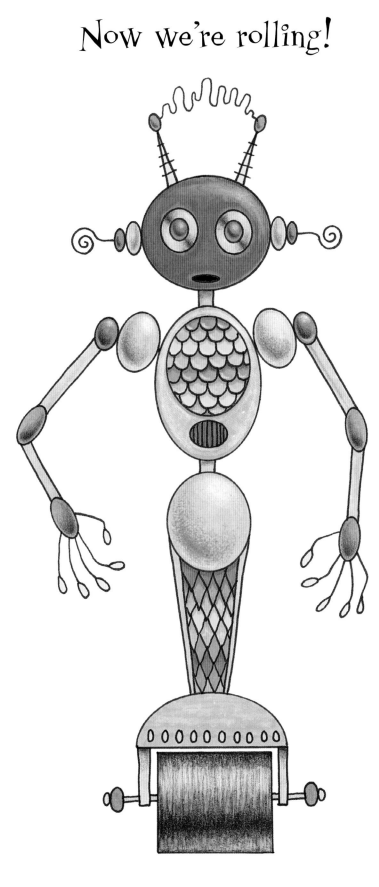

marker, watercolor, and colored pencil

Bellybot

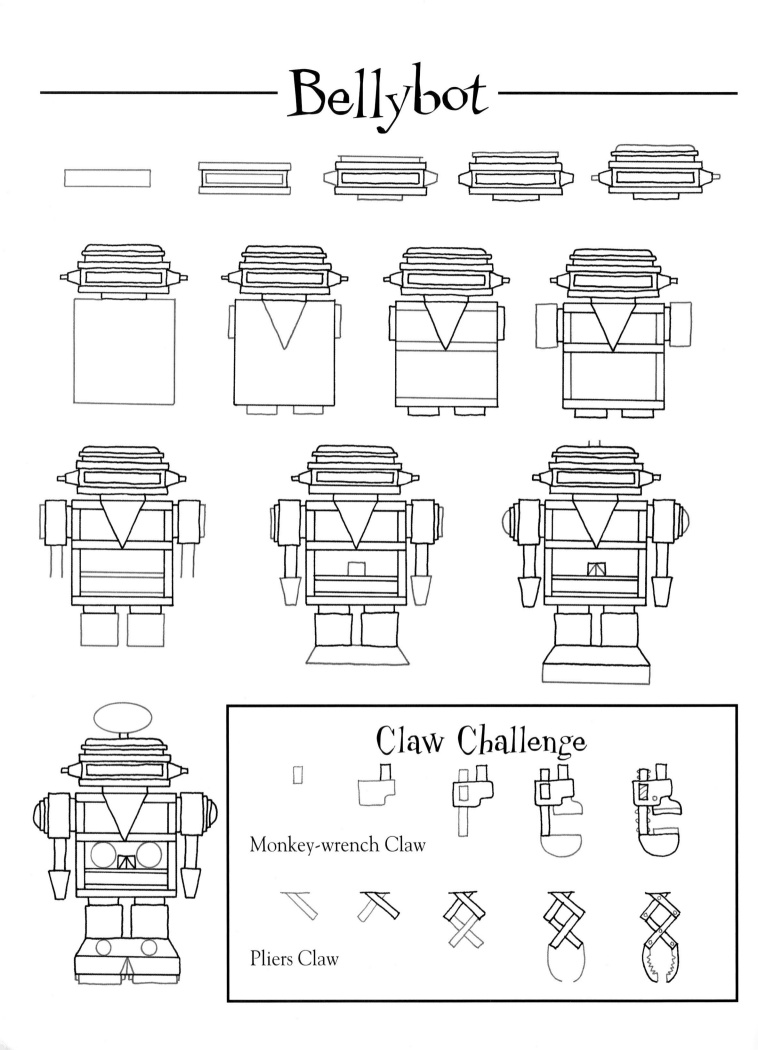

Claw Challenge

Monkey-wrench Claw

Pliers Claw

A robot's face can be anyplace.

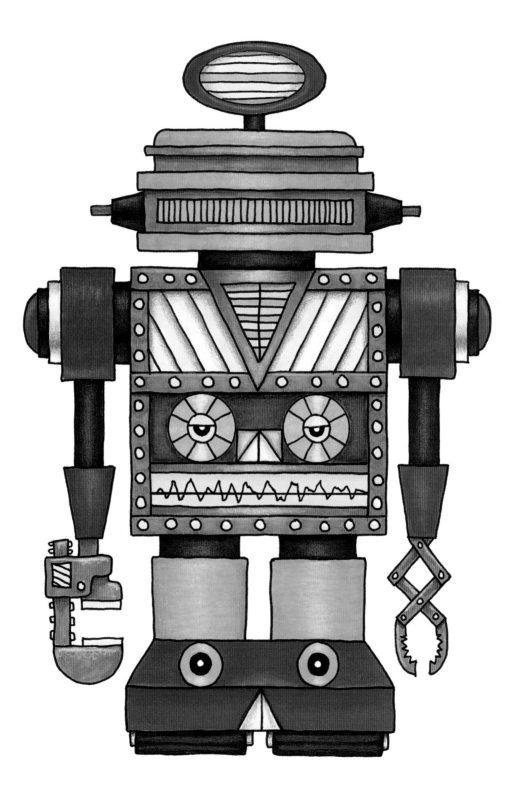

marker, colored pencil, and crayon

Walking TinCanBot

One small step for a robot,
one giant leap for robotkind.

marker, watercolor, and colored pencil

– Robot Assembly Line –

Build a mechanized family of fantastic bots!

Resources

Now that you've entered the fascinating world of robots, maybe you'd like to read more about them and possibly even build your own!

Books

For Younger Robot Fans

Carrick, Paul. *Watch Out for Wolfgang*. Watertown, MA: Charlesbridge, 2009.
> Three robot brothers must face Wolfgang the Recycler in this retelling of *The Three Little Pigs*.

Lucas, David. *The Robot and the Bluebird*. New York: Farrar, Straus and Giroux, 2007.
> A robot and a bluebird form an unlikely relationship in this book about love and friendship.

Riddell, Chris. *Wendel's Workshop*. New York: Katherine Tegen Books, 2010.
> Wendel, a wasteful inventor, must learn how to reuse and recycle in order to save himself from his own crazy robotic creation.

Yaccarino, Dan. *If I Had a Robot*. New York: Viking, 1996.
> Phil imagines what it would be like if he had a robot to eat his vegetables, do his homework, and feed the dog.

For Older Robot Fans

Domaine, Helena. *Robotics*. Minneapolis, MN: Lerner Publications Company, 2006.
> Read all about robots, from their history to their present use and future potential.

McComb, Gordon, and Myke Predko. *Robot Builder's Bonanza*. New York: McGraw-Hill, 2006.
> This is a great book for those who wish to build their own real robots!

McComb, Gordon. *Robot Builder's Sourcebook*. New York: McGraw-Hill, 2003.
> If you need parts to build your own robot, this book will definitely point you in the right direction.

Websites

Websites can change. Try running a search for robot on your favorite search engine.

For Younger Robot Fans

4²eXplore: Robots
http://42explore.com/robots.htm
This site provides some basic information about robots and includes tons of cool robot links to explore.

Highlights Kids: Make a Robot
http://www.highlightskids.com/Robot/h10robot.asp
If you've mastered drawing robots on paper, try building them electronically on this website.

Junior *FIRST* LEGO League
http://www.usfirst.org/roboticsprograms/jfll/
Overcome a scientific challenge with your team by building a creative solution with LEGOs.

For Older Robot Fans

Botball Educational Robotics
http://www.botball.org/
Work in teams to design and build robots for competitions.

Lawrence Technological University Robofest
http://www.robofest.net/
Learn science, engineering, technology, and math as you design and build robots for an annual competition.

NASA's Robotics Alliance Project
http://robotics.arc.nasa.gov/
Enter robotics competitions or find news and information about robots.

The Tech Museum: Robotics
http://www.thetech.org/robotics/
Read about robots, drive a simulated robotic vehicle, and view artwork inspired by robots. (Be sure to check out Clayton Bailey's life-size robotic sculptures!)